free to grow

by Madelaine Moss Koppelman
illustrated by Lenore Shaffer Koppelman

Free to Grow is a little story with a big meaning. The need for independence is universal. This book should be given as a gift to anyone who is afraid to take a much needed step toward healthy independence. It is also the perfect gift to give to someone who is standing in the way of another's independence. The book is written with so much love that the recipient will surely know that they are loved now, will be loved tomorrow and will always be loved.

Janet Ackerman

..[O]pen our circle of protection and give our kids healthier roots! This little book is a "must read" for parents at home and at parent support groups!

Cheryl M.
Educator

"*Free to Grow* is creative light reading and delicately illustrates the importance of space in any loving relationship. Sometimes in relationships giving space to another seems scary or threatening and *Free to Grow* is very helpful in explaining these feelings to a loved one by use of analogy! A must read!"

Beverly J. Mandell, M.S.

Maddy Koppelman wrote this brilliantly simple story to improve her own relationship. The words hit the right chords.. Do you know someone who could benefit by "letting go" a little? Please give them this book. *Free to Grow* could be titled *Letting Go.*

Marjorie Ventura
Educator

Alternate titles: "The Growing Tree" and "The Baby Tree"

Layout, typography and cover design by Steve Koppelman, www.heyboy-heygirl.com

Library of Congress Cataloging-in-Publication data is available.

ISBN: 978-1-4357-0761-0

www.freetogrowbook.com

For Samantha and Jack.
We love you so so so so so so MUCH!

This book is dedicated to my overprotective husband, Marc.
Thank you for growing with me all these years.

Acknowledgments

Steve, thank you for finding Lenore.
Lenore, thank you for finding Steve.
Cousin Lynn, thank you for the nagging and cajoling.
Tara and Andy, thank you for not nagging.
Pat Cohen, thank you for asking "why?"

Thank you for helping me to come from there to here: Cheryl Moss, Diane Zagare, Dr. and Mrs. Leo R. Schwartz, Bonnie Vandenberg, Claire Goldenberg, Irene Greenleaf, Susan and Manny Finer, Ruth and Arthur Brooks, Gail Rubenstein, Darlene and Howard Sydney, Darya and Larry Adler, Michelle Silver, Baron Brooks, Dr. Jay and Robin Gross, Steve and Kerri Tauber, Jack and Thelma, Aunt Dotty, Uncle Harry, Aunt Claire, Aunt Libby, the Milecofsky clan, Jo and Joe DeRosa, Adam and Eve, Amy and Jay, Deb Stiewing, Dr. Jeff Baron, Sybil Goodman, Dr. and Mrs. Randolph Brooks, Betty Lou Davis, Dr. and Mrs. Robert Markowitz, Sid Cohen, Lou and Janet Ackerman, Keith and Carrie Landis, Ivan and Lois Hubscher, Ellen and Richard Berliner, Ellen and Arthur Gold, Mary Ellen and Dave Olson.

free to grow

Once upon a time, there was a baby tree.

The baby tree lived in a forest with many other trees growing all around her.

Some of the trees were very old.

The old trees were very strong.

Their roots were planted firmly in the earth.

Their tall trunks

were thick

and gnarled

with age.

Their branches were so HIGH

that baby tree thought they could touch the SKY!

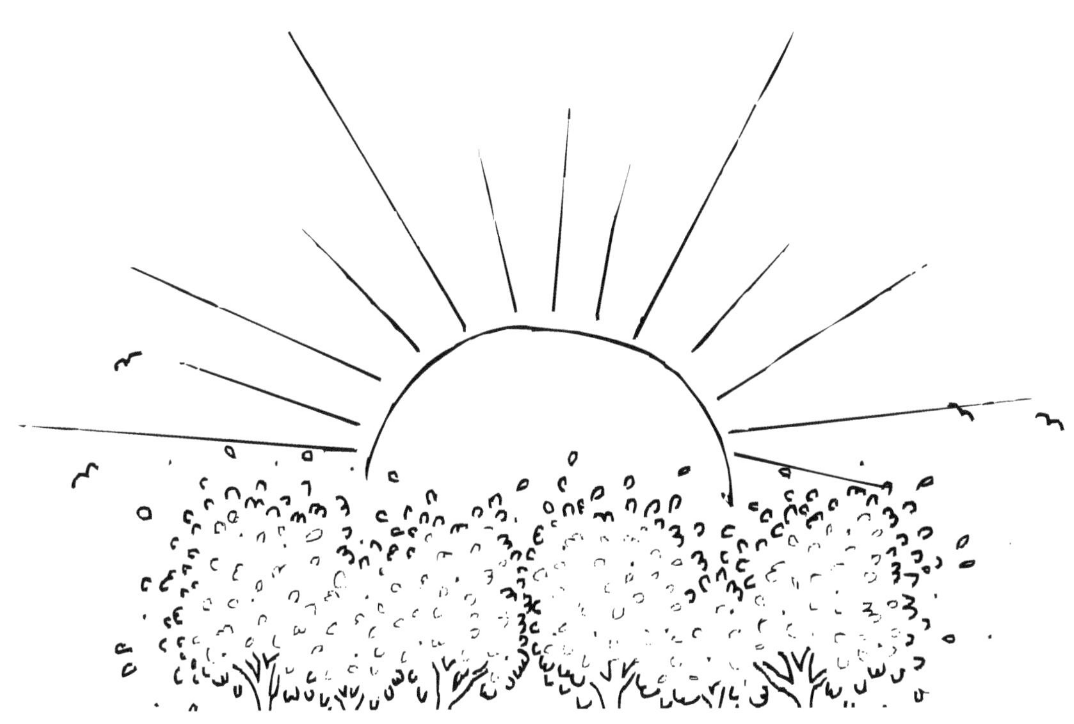

And their leaves were as glorious
as a golden crown.

The baby tree loved the big old trees
and the big old trees loved the baby tree.

When the baby tree was very tiny,
the big old trees protected her.

In the spring, they protected her young, frail trunk from the woodpeckers.

They said to the woodpeckers,
"Come peck on our big, strong trunks!
Let our baby tree grow!"

In the summer,

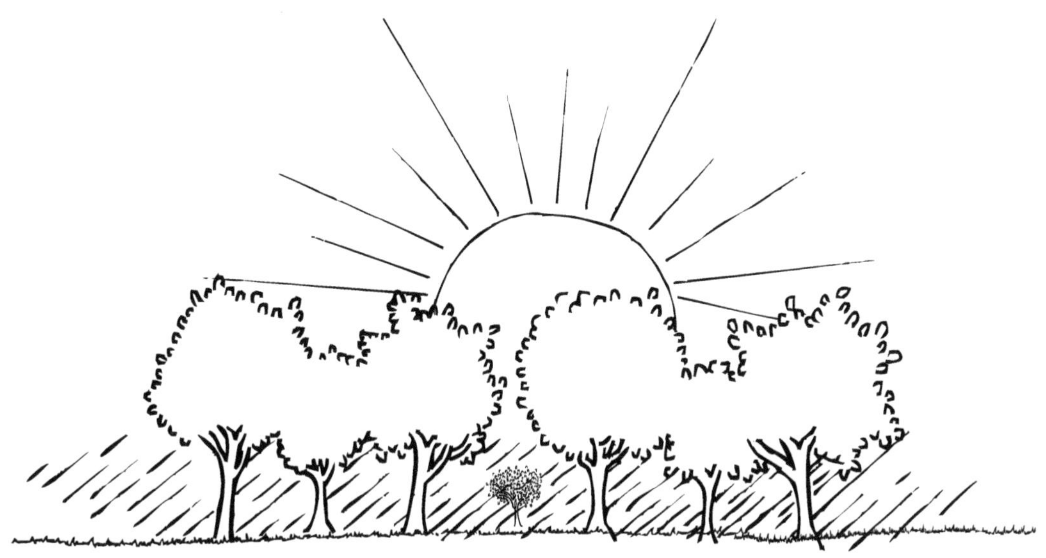

the tall, old trees
protected the baby tree
from the hot, burning sun.

In the fall,

the big old trees dropped their leaves onto the ground
to protect the baby tree.

The blanket of leaves kept the baby tree's roots warm
all winter.

And all through the winter, the strong old trees
kept the baby tree close inside their circle.

They protected her from the gusts of wind
that might have knocked her down.

After some time, the baby tree 

started to grow a little taller 

and a little stronger. 

She looked up at the trees around her...

“I want to be tall and strong like you,”
she said to them one day.

“You will, baby tree, you will”, they whispered.

Baby tree smiled as she stood in the circle of their love.
She felt safe.

She felt happy.
She was happy to know that she would grow up to be
just like them,

strong and tall and old.

Springtime came again and her family and friends

protected her from the woodpeckers.

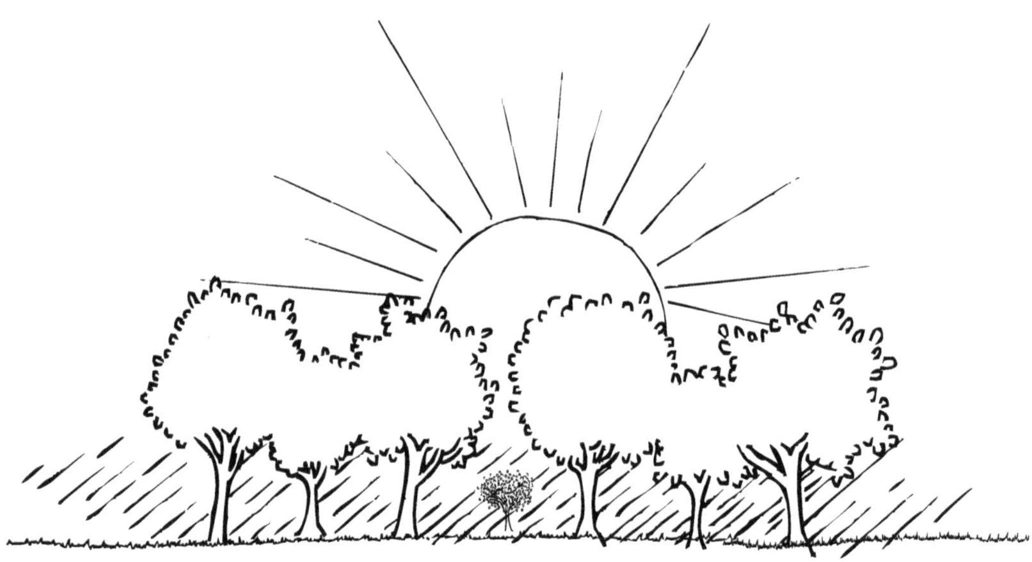

Summer came again

and her friends and family protected her
from the heat and the sun.

Fall came again

and her loved ones protected her
from the cold.

Winter came again

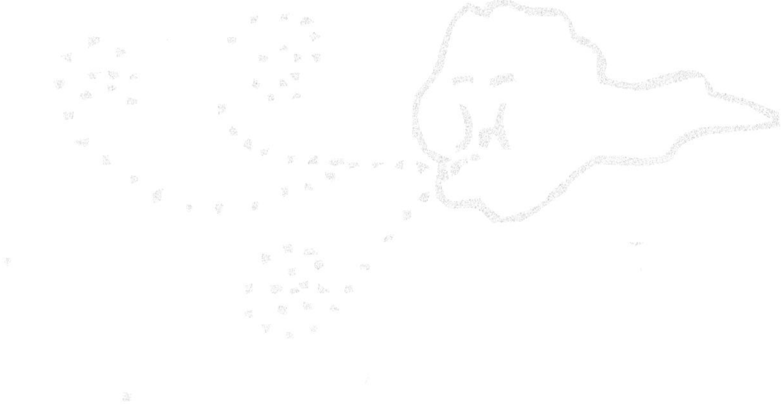

and everyone who loved her protected her from the wind.

One day, baby tree looked up at her friends.
She wanted to see how much she had grown.

“Oh dear!” she thought. She had not grown at all that year!

She did not feel strong.
She did not have many leaves on her branches.
Her branches did not reach upwards towards the sky.
Her branches drooped down towards the ground.

She looked down at her roots.

Her roots were tangled in the roots of the larger trees.
Her roots had no room to grow!

Baby tree started to think.

She thought about what she must do
to help herself grow.

She had to find a place with enough space
for her roots to grow deep enough
to improve her health.

She had to find a place
where the sun could shine on her leaves

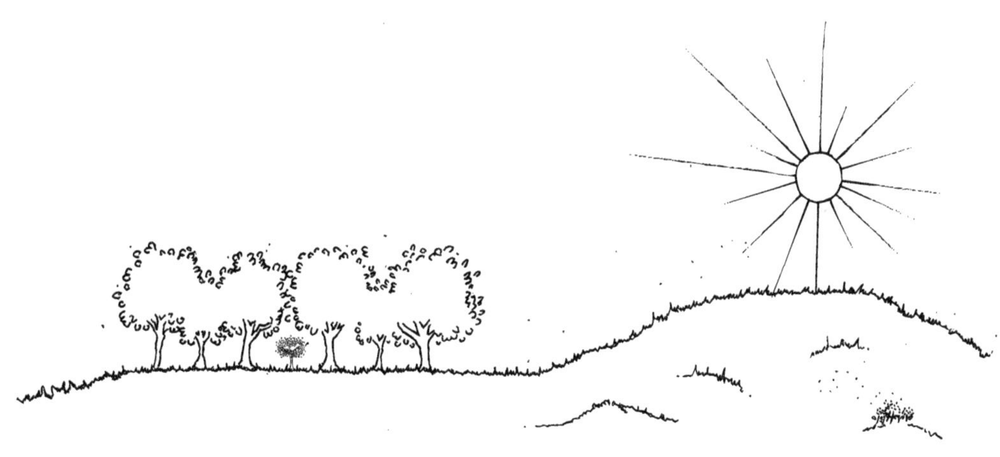

and encourage her branches to reach for the sky.

She had to find a place where she could stand straight and tall against the cold winter wind.

In such a place, she would be able to breathe.

In such a place she could grow strong.

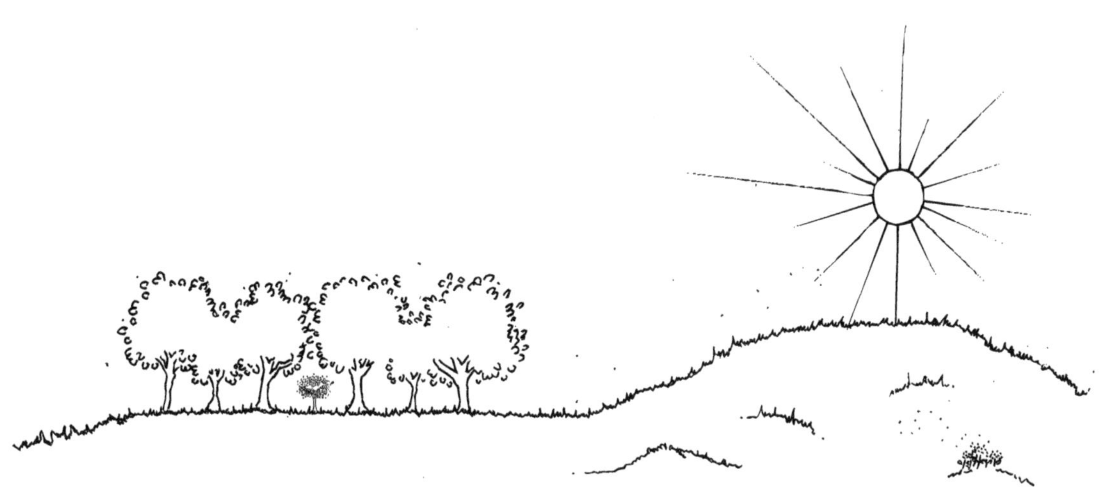

"But these trees are my family!" thought the baby tree.

"These trees are my friends! I would be so sad if I couldn't see them anymore! They would be so sad if they couldn't protect me anymore!"

The baby tree cried.

When she finished crying, she started thinking.

When she finished thinking, she knew with all her heart that she must have space to grow.

She also knew that she must have sunlight to grow.

She knew that without space and without sunlight, she would die.

With tears in her eyes, the young tree told her tall, old, dear friends that she was sick.

With pain in her heart, she told her strong, old, dear family that she must go away to find her own place in the sun.

The tall trees listened to the little tree.

The little tree listened to the big trees.

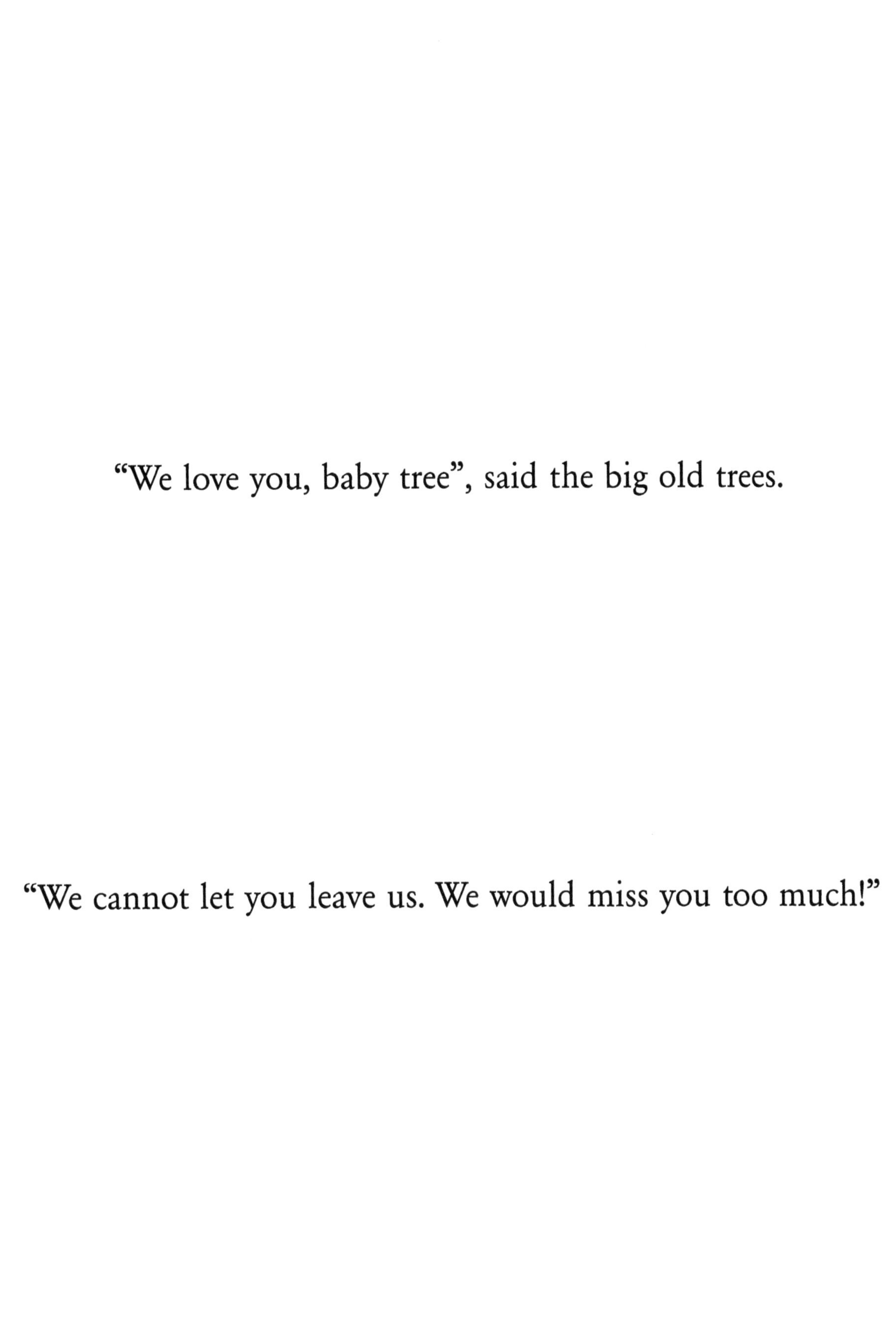

"We love you, baby tree", said the big old trees.

"We cannot let you leave us. We would miss you too much!"

“I will miss you too because I love you so much,” said the baby tree. “But if I am to live to be big and strong and tall like you,

I must leave this sheltered circle.”

The baby tree cried.

The big trees cried.

One big old tree stopped crying long enough
to ask the little tree,
“Why must you go so far away from us?”

“Far away from you?” sobbed the baby tree.
“I could never go far away from you!”

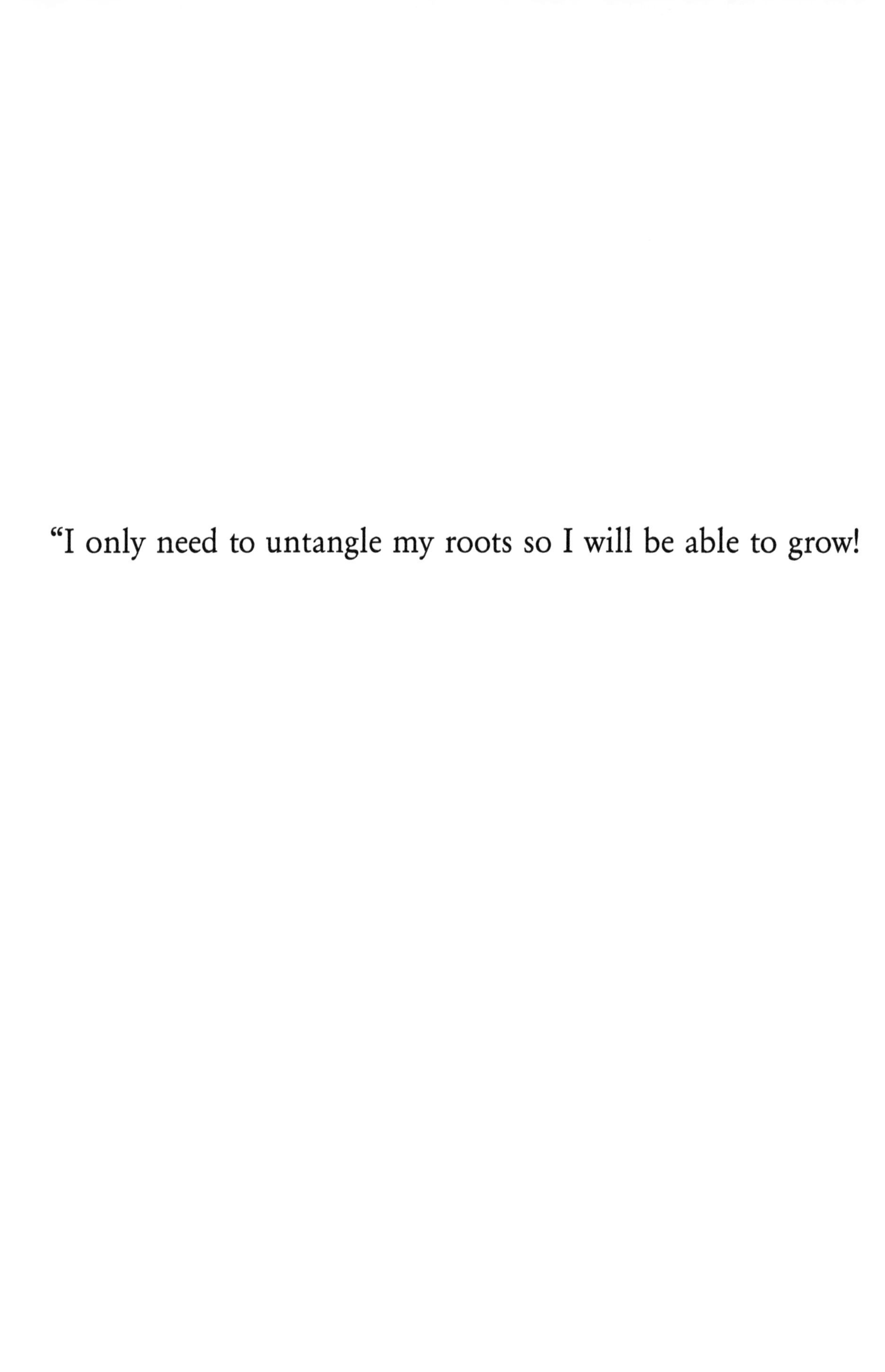

“I only need to untangle my roots so I will be able to grow!

Do you see that place over there?”

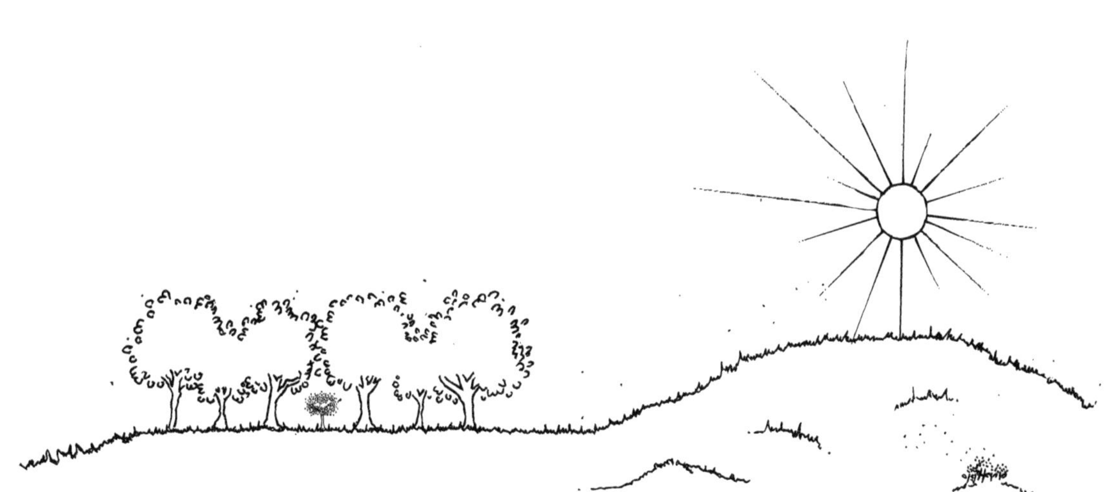

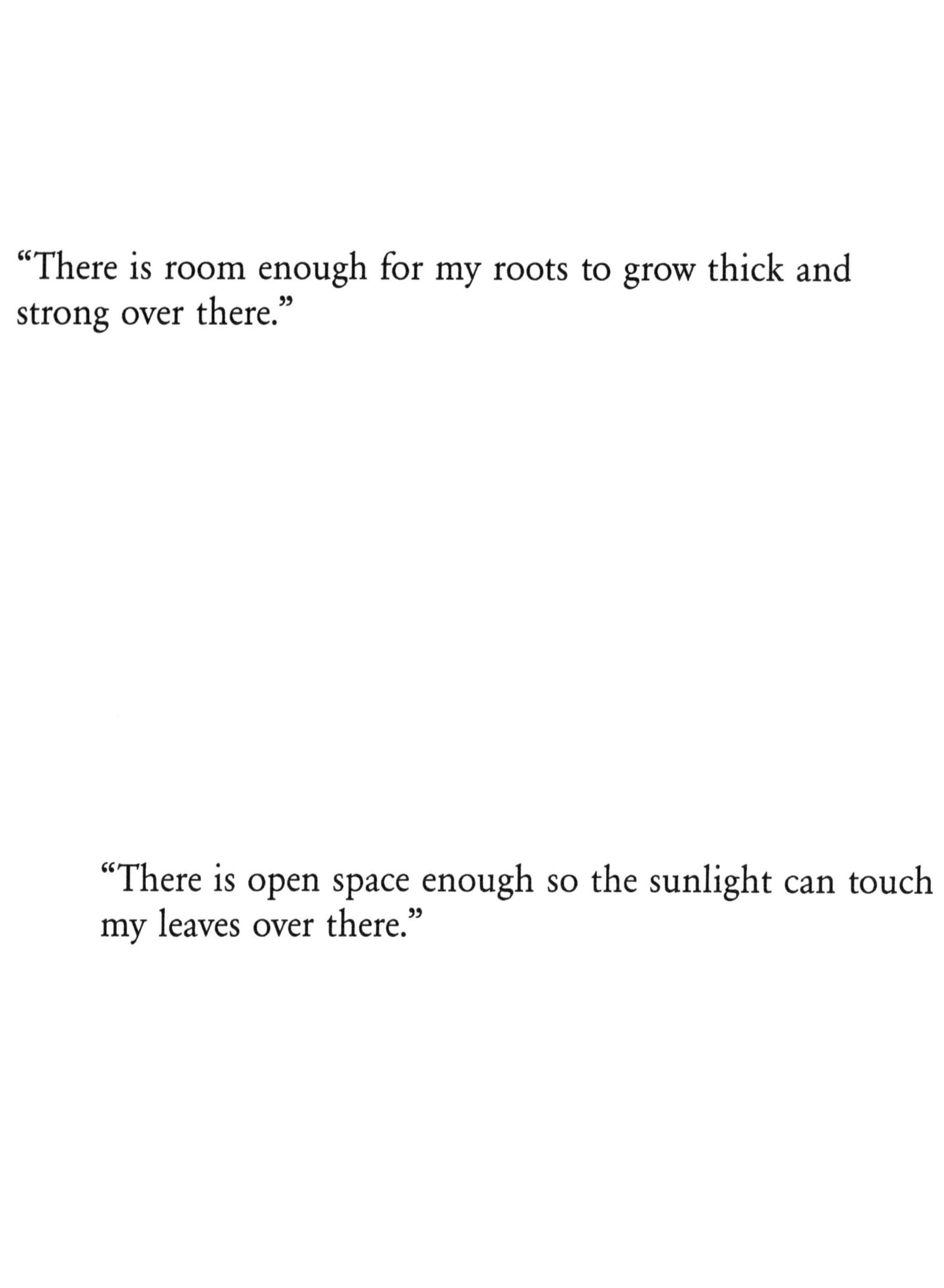

"There is room enough for my roots to grow thick and strong over there."

"There is open space enough so the sunlight can touch my leaves over there."

"But most important of all:
I will be able to see all of you

from over there!"

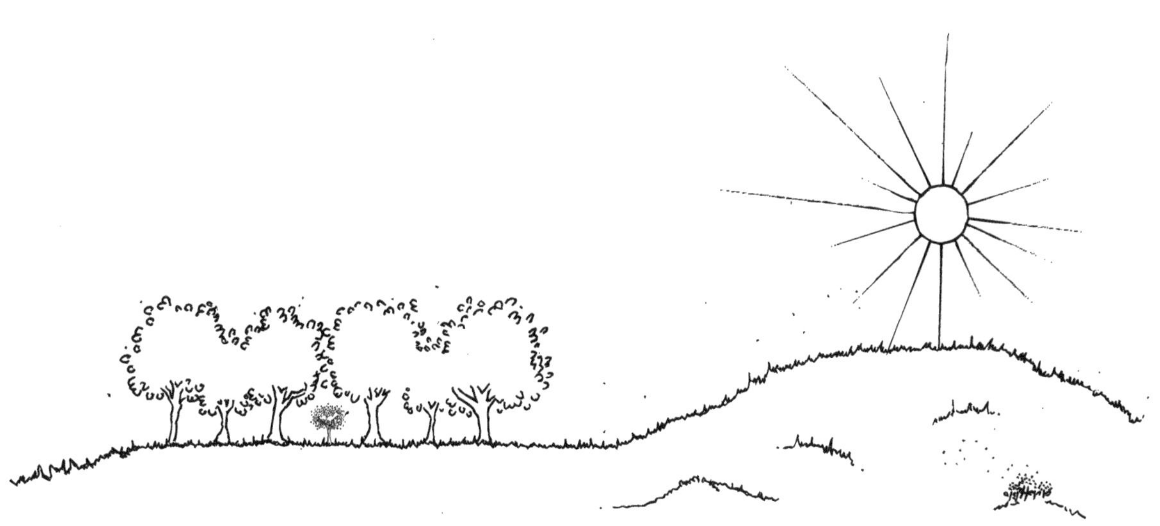

Suddenly the leaves stopped moving.
All was quiet for a moment.

Then the big, tall, strong old trees started crying again!
But this time they were crying with joy!

"If you could see us from over there,
then, we could see you from over here!"

"We will still be able to watch you grow!
You won't be very far from us after all!"

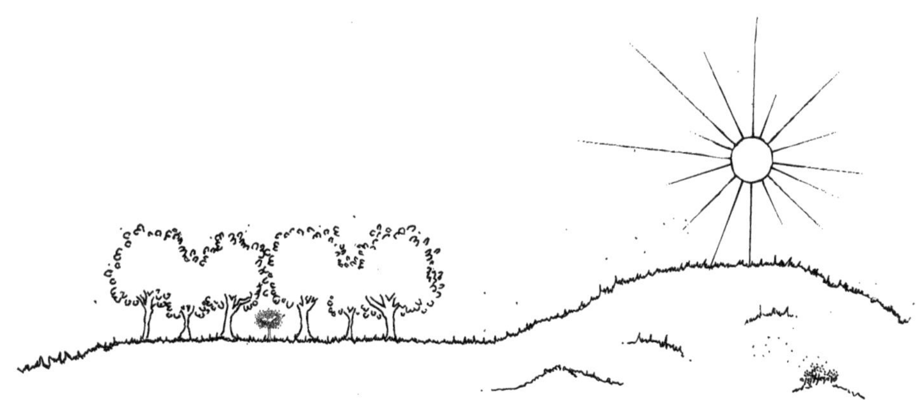

The little tree laughed.

The big trees laughed.

Then they all worked together to untangle
the baby tree's roots.

They had to be very careful.
They had to be very gentle.

It took a long time to separate the baby tree's tiny roots
from the big roots of the older trees.

All the family members and all the friends
had to work together
so no one would get hurt.

Everybody helped.

They all wanted the job done right

and it was done right.

Some years have passed since the trees got their roots untangled.

If you look up the hill you can see those big, tall, strong, old happy trees still standing together in their circle.

And if you just look a little further up the hill,

not too far away from the big, tall, strong, old happy trees...

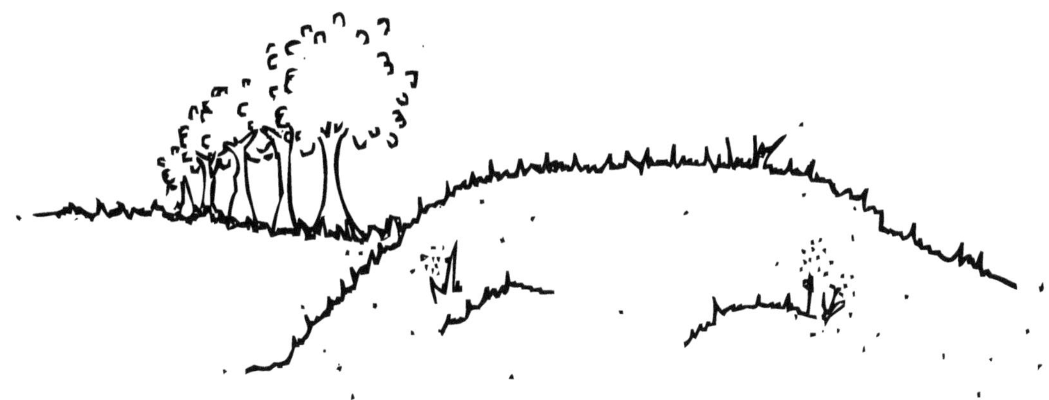

You can see a strong, young, happy tree,
that used to be
a frail, little baby.

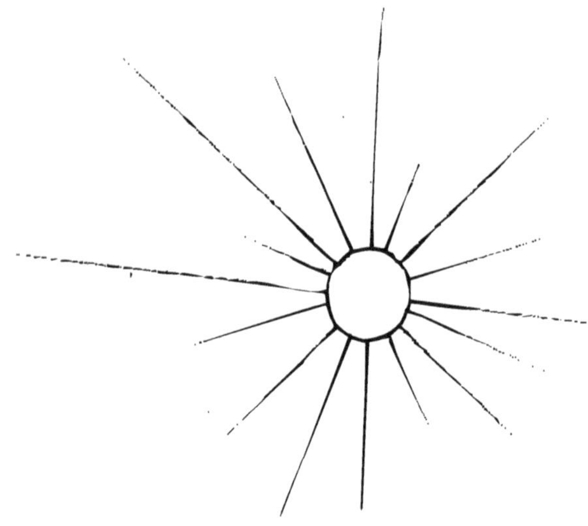

Afterword

When I was a young woman, my husband did a lot of traveling for his job. One day, I told him that I was planning to drive to my sister's house with our children and stay overnight. He wouldn't be home for the next two nights and I wanted to use this opportunity to visit my sister.

"You can't drive to New York by yourself", he said.

"Why not?"

"I'd worry about you too much," he said, " and I wouldn't be able to concentrate on my work. It wouldn't be fair to me."

"Okay," was my answer.

I stayed home with the kids that weekend in the quiet little town to which we'd recently moved. I was not happy but I did what he wanted me to do.

When I mentioned to friends or my sister that I didn't think I could go here or there because he wouldn't want me to, their reactions were raised eyebrows and disapproval of the way he was treating me. Their negative comments about the man I loved made me uncomfortable. My friends and my sister stopped asking me to join them. Still, I thought about it. I didn't know who was right and who was wrong, but I did know one thing for sure. I was not happy.

I thought I should have the freedom that most adults enjoyed and I wanted him to understand that if he "allowed" me to go, I would be a happier woman and that would be better for all of us.

I tried so many times to explain how I felt. He always turned it around to how *he* felt and how *his* feelings were more important because his need to concentrate on his job was important for us all.

I had to find a way to reach him. I was desperate to find a way to make him hear and understand me.

After much thought, I started to write a non-threatening, love-filled, gentle tale about a baby tree. This little tree would be so loved and protected by the other trees that the tree would have no room to grow. The tree might die of suffocation. I was careful and deliberate with each word, each comma. It took some time to re-work the words until I was satisfied with the message and how it would be perceived when he read it.

When I was finally satisfied that the story explained how I felt but would not hurt his feelings, I typed it up neatly and waited for the right opportunity to give it to him.

One evening, after the kids fell asleep, I told him that I needed to explain my feelings about our differing points of view. I told him that I had written this little story to explain how I felt and that maybe, after reading it, we might be able to talk about our differences in a new way.

He shrugged his shoulders and said “Okay.”

We sat down on the couch next to each other, shoulders touching. I sat still and silent as he read it to himself. I remember my heart was beating so loudly in my chest that I wondered if he could hear it. When he finished reading it, he turned to me with tears in his eyes.

“I never realized that I made you feel like that,” he said. “I wish I understood sooner. I’m so sorry I made you unhappy. I won’t let my worry get in the way of your freedom.”

When I told a few close friends what my story had accomplished in my relationship with my husband, some asked me if they could read it. I was surprised to learn that other people could relate to my complicated feelings associated with “letting go” and “letting grow”. I thought I was alone. I was wrong.

Over the years, this little story has been pulled out of the drawer and shared with people who have used it to break an impasse in their own relationships with family and with friends. With their urging and encouragement, I decided to publish this story.

My family, my friends and I all hope your life is enriched after you have read this gentle little book.

Dear Reader:

Please let me know if this book has helped you in your relationships.

If you belong to a book club and you would like me to participate in your discussion of this book at your meeting, contact me at:

www.freetogrowbook.com

I'd love to hear from you!

Maddy

www.ingramcontent.com/pod-product-compliance
Ingram Content Group UK Ltd.
Pitfield, Milton Keynes, MK11 3LW, UK
UKHW051128260726
13967UKWH00010B/2927